Patricia Beynen

Other books by the same Author

Non-Fiction for Older Adults, and those interested in such

- The Big R 1, The Life that Starts the Day After the Retirement Party
- The Big R 2, Using Your Time
- 50 Great Topics for Older Adult Discussion Groups (with Doris Grubin)
- 50 Great Skits for Older Adult Discussion Groups

Creative Non-Fiction

- My Life in Lincoln, Bathsheba Brooks Fiske, 1789-1872
- The 1910 Diary of May Fitzsimmons

Fiction for Late Middle Grade and Young Adult

- Goldmine House
- My Dutch Summer
- Breathing Space
- Checking In: Getting Through Covid

Patricia Beynen

ISBN: 9798752197734

Imprint: Independently published

Printed in the United States of America

Patricia.Beynen@gmail.com

Thank you to two writing groups full of excellent commenters: Norm, Lee, Ann, Barb, Conrad, Emily, Tony, and Lynn. I so appreciate the thought you put into your suggestions. To my "Oldish Women's Group" who were always interested in the book progress, and were willing walking partners. And of course, to Bert, who was the soul of encouragement from the first moment I told him the name of the book, before a word was written.

Patricia Beynen

But the walking of which I speak has nothing in it akin to taking exercise, as it is called, as the sick take medicine at stated hours,--as the swinging of dumb-bells or chairs; but is itself the enterprise and adventure of the day.

---Henry David Thoreau

Patricia Beynen

CONTENTS

Patricia Beynen

Patricia Beynen

The Elder's Guide to Genteel Walking

Introduction

Genteel walking is more of a pastime than a sport. It's not competitive, and the goals are to see nice views, breathe some fresh air, perhaps spend time with a friend, while getting the benefits of movement for all your body parts. And you can do it without spending a dime. It gentler than hiking, definitely kinder than running, and more cheerful than the gym.

Settling in on the sofa is so easy. Puttering around the house and garden. Taking the car out to have lunch with a friend, see the grandchildren, or picking up a book from the library can fill a day. Shopping used to be a way to get out and about but the pandemic has made many of us on-line shoppers, even for groceries. The sitting, puttering, driving, on-line shopping life may be convenient, but it's not so good for our long-term prospects of health and mobility.

I was thinking of the elder woman as I wrote. I imagined myself talking to her as we made our way around the park. But on proper reflection why only for women? Do men not age and retire to too many hours in their recliners? Walking is for everybody. No age requirements, no gender identity needed.

Remember when calling someone elder meant really old? Now that we are them, or at least I am, I'd like to reclaim the term elder. For a while I saw it as a marker of the decrepit, falling-down old. Not so much anymore. I like the association with The Elders, the wise group of older people who are consulted for their

wisdom. Not that I am consulted for my wisdom, but it's

a good association. I also am seeing the decrepit, falling-

down old with kinder and more self-identifying eyes.

Oh, right, falling, I've done that, but lived to tell about it,

and I'm ok. Decrepit? Eye of the beholder. There's still a

person behind those wrinkles.

Walking is offered by our medical establishment,

like the Mayo Clinic, as the antidote for a lot of ills, for

example improving your energy levels, muscle

endurance, sleep, balance, cardio fitness, and a healthy

weight. Plus, plus.

Even as I felt like I was an advocate for older

adults, my previous preferred term, I did harbor some

dismissive notions about couch potatoes. Perhaps not as

active as before, not taking classes, volunteering,

mentoring, nor carrying on with many of their early retirement interests. The sofa had become too comfortable.

Some of us have been lifelong exercisers. Belonged to hiking clubs and gyms. Played tennis. Swam. Danced with vigor. Ran for fun, marathons even. Not me.

What I do is walk. Not all that much, and until recently not particularly planned, but I did walk. I have three basic kinds of walks which I'll talk more about, but it gives a little variety to what can be a boring way to spend some time.

The hardest part is getting off the sofa. Let's start there.

Up From the Sofa

Let me guess. You're waiting for the magic to happen. You've read this far, and have hopes that there is a special sequence of events that will happen if only…if only you say the right words, find the right spot, wear the right shoes, get in the right frame of mind, confide in the right person. I could go on. Maybe it's true. I've heard people say the only way they can get a bulky old car started is if they slam the door, turn on the heater, wait 30 seconds, jam their foot on the brake and turn the key. Like that, the magic happens, and the car starts. Otherwise, nada.

OK, here's step one. Put on decent shoes, the ones you wouldn't mind wearing on an every-aisle trip to the grocery store. Step two: What are you wearing? Pants, a tee shirt and a sweater? Fine. You might want to tie the sweater around your waist later, but fine for now. Shorts, skorts, a skirt, a dress, capris…they're all fine as long as you're comfortable. Step three, check your pockets, you need some ID, and your Medicare/health insurance card. That's my irreducible minimum. A cell phone is nice too, and a five-dollar bill. Step four, how's the weather? Not raining or sleeting? Put on appropriate layers. You're good. Step five, destination? Out your front door is the easiest, so let's do that today. You pick, left or right. Check the time. Good, you're off.

Just walk, like you're on the way to the bus, but not in a rush. Watch your footing, like you usually do. You probably know this sidewalk very well, know where the tree roots are, the crumbling cement. Take care, like always. Look around. The same houses you see every day? Pick one feature like, say, doorways, and compare.

See any good ones? Something that makes the whole

entryway look better. What are the elements that make it

look good? By the time I figure that out I've gone by two

more houses. Pick anything that interests you.

Driveways, curtains, flowers. Even not-so-nice things

like trash, places needing repairs, where some touch up

paint would make a difference. Now check the time.

Have 10 minutes gone by? If so, cross the street and start

back home, keeping up your observations. There, you're

home, you've done your first 20-minute walk. Good for

you. Have something to drink. For me it's iced tea in the

warm months, hot tea in the cold.

Keeping a journal will help. You're only going to

write a few lines a day, so anything small will do, even

one of those little monthly calendar planners that come

in the mail as advertisements. You want to have the date,

the amount of time you spent walking, anything of significance to remember, like, say, #321 has a pretty doorway, how far you got, or you're out of breath, or that was easy. Your choice, but you'll be glad you wrote it later. If you've already started using a step counter, note the number.

Were you absolutely done in, barely able to function for an hour after you got back? OK, let's back you off to 10 minutes total, five out, five back. Or, were you sorry it was over, could have gone longer? OK, 15 out, and 15 back for you tomorrow. Maybe you were slightly out of breath, but pretty fine, really. Good, do it again tomorrow, same timing. You see where I'm going with this. It's very mama bear, papa bear. Not too long, not to short, but just right. If you're new to walking, ten plus ten is usually just right.

The timing will change as we get into this but for now, find just right, and keep with it for one week.

Look at you. Off the sofa.

If you want a daily plan for eight weeks, check the appendix. It's the "Just tell me what to do" approach. Either way, the daily plan, or reading on for lots of ways and reasons to walk, **it's a good idea to talk to your doctor and tell them what you want to do**. Ask if there's any medical reason why you shouldn't start walking every day, increasing your daily steps to 3000, and maybe more. Listen to what s/he says. Is there a medical reason not to walk daily? Rarely, but always good to ask.

Patricia Beynen

Why Bother?

Because you don't want to be helpless, you want to maintain your mobility. The more you sit, the less you move, the more capability you lose. It's insidious, isn't it? You, who used to have such an active life, now find small acts challenging. Getting up from a comfortable chair isn't comfortable. You want to be independent, able to do for yourself.

What does your personal picture look like if the direction you're going continues? Are you more or less able than you were a year ago? If it's less able, why? Sure, lots of possible reasons. Gained weight, been sick or injured, pandemic-required house confinement, another year older.

You're not helpless here.

You probably know already what you can do about most of that. Think healthy food, physical therapy, and planned outdoor time, but the "another year older" part? What's a person to do?

Don't take it lying down, that's what. Sure, sure, we'll all come to that inevitable end, but let's not go quietly, OK? Let's do what we can to keep it together, be independent, do the best we can with body, mind, and spirit.

Have you seen the exercises the Federal government publishes for older adults? I've done them in classes at a senior center, and they're fine, good for you. But boring, and for me they require a class and instructor. The workout is available on the internet and anyone can do them at home, but, boring. For me, boring means good intentions aren't enough, and it all fades away. I want to keep the body moving, but exercise classes are apparently not sufficient motivation. I want to be more in charge of the time and place, the length of time, the pace, and the company, or lack thereof. Also, I want the reward of seeing progress.

When I'm spending time with our younger generations, they kindly slow their pace for me, and constrain the activity options to an easier subset. I'd like to slow the direction that's going in. When a walk through a pretty, and large, park is an option I want to say "yes," not "well, for a little way." They do amazing things, travel and climb and canoe. I'll cheer them on. But I'd like to say "Let's go for a walk," and keep up a decent pace.

Not to mention being prepared for an emergency. I read a story once about Noah, and Mrs. Noah. They were not young, already the parents of adults, and lifespans are much longer today than in antiquity. They were faced with an enormous task, building that ark, navigating through the storm and flood, keeping the animals and humans alive, then starting again. For that you need stamina, strength, good bones, and a functional cardio vascular system. Seems they did fine. Be like Noah, and Mrs. Noah.

Patricia Beynen

Shoes

I haven't bought any new shoes for walking, but you can. In the warm weather I either wear my very comfortable sandals, or some "walking shoes" I've had in the closet for a few years. Bigger than sneakers, with a broader foundation, white with laces. I look like I'm getting down to business. I usually do wear them on trail walks, although some of my friends wear ankle-supporting walking boots at such moments.

In colder weather I wear my last year's version of this year's shoe. I've worn the same zip up shoe with rubber soles for the last few years for everyday wear, but after they get a little battered looking, they become my walking shoes, and I don't care if they get even more battered looking. If it's snowy or icy out I have a stouter pair of boot-like shoes previously used for clearing off the car and snow shoveling. If it's icy out I don't walk much, maybe just on city sidewalks that have been salted, maybe just to the car, then the coffee bar.

But you do you. If you like a good excuse to buy task-specific shoes, here's your moment. If the closet candidates aren't up to the job, wear the best of the lot for a walk or two and see what you think. Old or new you need some decent support, protection from the elements, and if having specific shoes for walking is motivating, then new shoes for you. Style, newness, color, and specific shape are not requirements.

Patricia Beynen

Routes

I'm up to about a dozen routes now, in three
types.

Neighborhood

My most common, everyday way of walking.
Out the door, left or right, to the corner, left or right, and
so on. I've done it so many times that I know, mostly,
what awaits me. Which way has a daunting hill, that in
the early days I only walked down, and now I walk up.
The one with the truly terrible sidewalks overgrown with
tree roots, never swept of leaves, and horribly uneven. I
still walk several of those, but I never take my eyes off
the ground, prepared for the place the tree roots have
grown through the sidewalk, making a jagged peak to get
around. We also have a lot of brick sidewalks here in this

old section of Philadelphia. Pretty to look at, but can be treacherous if not well maintained.

Ease of walking is one thing, but what do I want to see today? I can get to a big, foresty park if I want a woods walk, or a neighborhood park if I want some pretty flowers, and cute kids on the playground. Do I want to swing by the historic section? The rich people's houses? Or maybe today is my day to look down driveways for those old carriage houses I think are so great. Sometimes it's a destination walk, with the library, or coffee, a restaurant, or a friend's house my end goal.

Trail Walks

Philadelphia is blessed with a lot of parks, with trails, and we also have old, closed, railroad lines now made into trails. During the worst of the pandemic shutdown the city closed some streets, especially along a river, and designated them as no-car, walking and biking areas.

Trails are usually companion walks for me. A chance to walk and talk and catch up. Trails, especially the woodsy and railroad trails can be isolated, empty places, and it's nice to have somebody else along. Not that either of us would be intimidating to any would-be bad guy, but it seems smarter. Going for one of these walks can be a social occasion. They might involve coffee or lunch, but usually not. Walking is enough. Bring water for a break along the trail at the halfway mark.

The City Walk

By city I mean downtown, tall buildings, the where-it's-happening area. I rarely drive downtown since I have a train stop near me which, pre-pandemic, was a dependable way to get into Center City, as downtown is called here. Not so dependable at the moment because of reduced scheduling, but at least it's back after being shuttered for more than a year. No commuters, no commuter train.

My point, though, is that a city downtown is a delightful place to walk, especially if you're out of the immediate shadow of the skyscrapers. Or maybe they're your thing. My favorite areas are the mixed ones, residential, commercial, and little parks. Lots to see, and consider. Let's look at that menu in the window, or a dress being displayed, or a thrift shop, or the way the homeowner decorated that stoop. So much to see. No matter how many times I've been down those cobblestones I still see something new. I don't have a fixed route, but I do keep in mind how far I'm walking from the spot I have to get back to, whether it's the subway stop, the place I left my people who decided more coffee was better than walking, or where I left the car. Getting too far ahead of my return capability can be stressful.

Another way I use Center City is to get off at the wrong stop, and walk from there to get in a walk either before or after something scheduled in the area.

Plus one more, a combo of the above.

The City/Neighborhood Hybrid

Here in Philadelphia people over 65 have free public transit on trains, buses, trolleys, and the subway. An incredible benefit, and one I have taken much advantage of in the past. It didn't completely go away during the quarantine, but it went away for me.

One fun way to use it is to find a friend who likes small adventures, take the train, bus, etc. to an unfamiliar place, perhaps the end of the line, do a walkabout in the area, have lunch, and retrace your path back home. Walking someplace unfamiliar is fun, a little challenging, and breaks the patterns.

Most cities have some form of subsidized senior transit, thanks to the Older Americans Act, so if it's unfamiliar to you, it's worth a look. Ours is subsidized by the state lottery, part of the plan for the lottery profits from the beginning, along with subsidizing other senior functions, like lunches at the Senior Centers.

Patricia Beynen

The People You Meet

Neighbors on your own street. My usual conversation with neighbors was when I was walking to my car, and giving conventional how-you-doing? type greetings, perhaps slowing my pace a tiny bit. I was on my way someplace, on the move. Now that I'm a walker the only place I'm headed is back home again, so I have lots of chat time. Maybe they don't, and are in their own "on my way" mode, which is certainly fine, but maybe they respond to my "What's new?" with a story of what's new. We had a tree taken down across the street, a huge tree that gave a lot of shade. Turns out that everybody had an opinion, mostly against, a few understanding the need, some with inside knowledge, and a universal sadness over the loss of that diseased and dangerous beauty. Potholes are another community bonding event. "Has anyone reported it?" with lots of repeat inquiries about the deficiencies in the city systems to deal with such issues. Now that I'm not in a rush to get to my car I have lots to say myself. We have a neighborhood with potlucks and mutual assistance, but it all needs to be nourished, by contact and conversation.

Dog walkers. These come in two types, the professional and the family walkers. I've gotten to know most of the dogs now, who are eager to make my acquaintance, actually anybody's acquaintance. They are all on leashes with observant handlers so they don't worry me. I occasionally run into them in the park where they are sometimes unleashed, chasing a ball. I can have the fun of flinging a ball from one of those anti-slobber holders, happily greet my eager furry friends, and not have a care in the world for carrying poop bags. Can you tell I don't have a dog at home? I have had dogs in the past, but now they seem like a lot of work. I'll take these small visits happily. A nice chance to catch up with their people as well. My current favorite dog walking encounter is an adult male walking a full-grown pit bull, along with his daughter, aged maybe four, maybe five, walking a pit bull puppy. They stop often, practicing commands, and I think they're all adorable. If you are the dogwalker yourself, we'll talk more about that in a minute.

Fellow travelers. Sturdy shoes, a determined pace, often a hat, comfortable weather-appropriate clothes, and no bags. Some are on strict schedules. Two white-haired women go by my corner at 8:10 every morning. Fellow walkers for sure. Another indicator is the earpiece, listening to a podcast, or maybe music.

We've become familiar to each other, say good morning without pausing, and are mutual parts of each other's landscape.

Chatters. I'm usually up for a good chat. I'm not trying to get 5000 steps in before eight AM so if someone I know stops me with their chat face on, I'm game. I've run into people I haven't seen since pre-pandemic, people I used to know in different settings and didn't even know they lived nearby, some who I knew lightly from common activities, some who are good friends who just happened to be sharing the same sidewalk at the moment. "Hi! How ya doing?" And so begins the catch up. It's all fun.

It's also all motivation. Sometimes as I'm trying to talk myself into getting up and out, I do wonder who I might encounter today. It's always a cheering thought,

and gives me a little push.

If You Have a Dog (or Even if You Don't)

Was there ever a better reason to get out there than those big sweet eyes looking at you, projecting the idea of a good romp? If you already have a dog, somebody is walking it. Maybe a shared responsibility with another family member, maybe you have a paid helper, or you do it all yourself. Or maybe you have a big fenced area where Fido's idea of a good time is to run around in circles.

Whatever your story, you have the number one best encouragement to put one foot in front of the other. If your dog is like mine was, the mere act of getting out the leash created dog excitement. "Yes! We're doing it! She's putting on her coat! Yay! C'mon!" I speak dog, and if it wasn't clear to you what Sweet Thing was saying, there's the translation of that jumping around after a leash sighting.

Now that we are in our more advanced years, the pace of these walks may have slowed some. The pace for an older dog may have also slowed. Taking all that into consideration, and bearing in mind that this is one of the highpoints of Charlie's day, you set the pace, and carry on. Once walking becomes a more welcome part of your day, you might want to take over more of the walks if it's been a shared responsibility. Or walk with the family member who you're sharing the responsibility with. Or walk longer and farther.

If you've been a sidewalk, poop-scooping walker, consider being a trail-walking, poop-scooping walker. New scenery, new smells, and new fellow walkers, human and canine. Taking off the leash to let the pup run is usually frowned on since 1) dogs get excited, run after a squirrel, and get lost, and 2) the other folks on the trail won't appreciate an unleashed dog. Dog parks are another story, but unless that's your destination after a good walk it's not the story here.

If all this sounds jolly, but you don't have a dog, think about borrowing one. People who already consider you trustworthy might be delighted to share the responsibility of walking Lil Poopsie whether once or more regularly. A break for them, fun and steps for you.

Or, consider this: Dog pounds/rescues are places filled with dogs who need exercise. You could volunteer to be their walker for a day or a month or forever. If it turns out you love it, but don't want the rest of the dog care issues that come with having a dog at home, that's great, your walks will mean a lot to these guys. But it if turns out having a dog at home seems like a good idea,

but not a good long-term idea, consider fostering one of

them. Win/win.

Count Your Steps

Not everyone loves this, but let me make a case in favor of the count.

Ages ago I had a step counter that was a separate gizmo, given by me by my employer to promote good health and no doubt keep their health insurance premiums down. The goal was to walk 10,000 steps every day, which is a lot, but it was the 90's and I was younger then. I lived in Iowa where the winters are fierce, and you'd think that would be an impediment, but no, I had the ideal walking situation. I worked in a building attached to the Des Moines skywalk system, a second-floor tunnel-like connection between buildings that kept the weather out, both hot and cold. With determination I could get in the 10K steps in one lunch hour, but it was more of a sprint and less of a lunch hour, so I was usually happy with six or seven thousand, and a peanut butter and marmalade sandwich. There was a reward for doing a certain number of steps in the duration of the program, which I don't remember ever winning. But it did establish some good habits for a while, and I found walking with other women to be something I enjoyed. The counting gizmo eventually stopped working, life moved on, and I didn't count steps again, until recently. I did time my walks during one weight loss journey to make sure I didn't quit too soon, before the twenty minutes was up.

Fast forwarding to more recent times, when everything we do seems to be connected to our cell phones, I now use a free step-tracker on my phone. It tells me steps, distance, time, and calories burned. I can also compete with other people, or create a map of my walk. Fancy stuff like that. But all I really want to know is how many steps I walked today.

I remember from my work life that a first step in improving performance is measurement. If your best performer makes 50 widgets in an hour, the average performer makes 35, and you've got a few that make five or six you've identified useful facts. First you want to reward Ms. Fifty Widgets, acknowledge the average people, and motivate all to improve. If you don't count you've got nothing to say, no way to know what's exceptional, a reasonable expectation, or what needs improvement. Throw in a few more measurables like length of time on the job, and error rates, and you can establish standards.

Patricia Beynen

So, what do us walkers want to know? The main thing that interests me is just the raw number. How many steps did I walk today? It's interesting. I relate it to how it felt. Am I worn out? Did it feel difficult at the time? What's different than yesterday? Where does this number fit in the trend?

For example, today I walked 2496 steps, which is once around the big block. Yesterday I walked 6708 steps, which took me many streets from home. I was happy with both numbers. Yesterday because that's a pretty big number for me. I've been up to 10K but that was over a whole day of tourist walking in another city, so not comparable to a neighborhood walk, and it was cooler yesterday than today. Today I considered not walking at all. I got a late start on the day, nobody was expecting me to walk with them, and it was hot. But

some is better than none, so I went around the big block.
There's also the little block, but I felt tougher than that.
I'm glad I did it, and don't have a tiny walking-around-
the-house-and-yard number on my tracker. If it wasn't
for the tracker I might have not walked at all, so good for
the tracker's motivational properties.

It's also a record, keeping track of the days since
I started using it. I can see how slow I used to be. If I
combine it with my calendar, I can identify the days I
walked with other people, which in the early days were
the only times I had numbers over 2K. Right there I see
good info…walking with a friend equals walking further.
Often those friend walks involved coffee or lunch in the
middle, giving me a chance to regroup before setting out
again.

Not to mention a little bit of fun. Something to announce when I get home. A number to marvel over when I do a long walk. A way to see improvement. For some people it might have a competitive element, but not for me. It's not a race, just a walk.

I understand that Fitbits and smart watches tell you all this, plus more. Sounds cool, but so far. I'm sticking with my free phone app.

Find a Companion, or a Group

I see them all the time. Pairs or groups of people walking, especially on the trails and paths. Last week I was walking on Forbidden Drive with a friend (cars are the forbidden item, and have been since this dirt road opened in the 1920's). Although it wasn't crowded like it gets on the weekend, there was a brisk amount of foot traffic. Groups of older women, or older men. Mothers and children, and mixed groups of women and children. Kids with a leader. They seem self-selected by gender and age, but that's only a guess. I know of a few groups from senior centers who walk with other folks from the center, and it seems it's only the women who sign up.

I've also seen postings on our community page on Facebook that a group leaves every morning from X corner at a certain time, and all are welcome to join. Joining only means showing up at that time and place. My church has an informal group who like to walk, and will send out an email about time, starting place, and destination. A lot of organizations seem to see walking as a way for people to get to know each other outside of a meeting. In fact, I once went to a corporate retreat in a beautiful place where the only meetings allowed had to be while walking.

You can always google it. I expect you'll get a list of groups from www.meetup.com. I got a few dozen categories, including bird walks, specific neighborhoods, some out of the city destination walks, a photo and walk group, an over 55 group. And on and on. Empty nesters, Girls-just-wanna-have-fun walking, All-things-dogs walkers. I'm not kidding. A LOT of groups. Beware of the word "hike" unless what you're really after is a hearty event at a brisk pace that goes on for several hours and involves hills, and special shoes. Those are not my people. Not even my gene pool. Lovely folk, I expect, but made of sterner stuff than I.

Or, more simply, just put the word out. Are you part of any groups now? Book clubs, religious groups, neighborhood organizations, political…anything. At your next meeting ask "Are any of you walkers? I'm a new recruit to the 'walking for the fun of it' world and go on my own most days, but would love to walk with one of you if we find a time that works." You'll get some fellow travelers for sure.

And what about your core group of friends, the people you have lunch with, and who know the first names of all the important characters in your life.

Patricia Beynen

Suggest a venue for lunch that has walking potential, which can be nearly anywhere from fancy downtown to a charming tea room in the suburbs to a specific place along a walking trail. Walk before or after lunch, or both. Make sure you mention the walking part ahead of time so no one shows up in inappropriate shoes. I find that most of my friends have long since ditched their inappropriate shoes for comfort shoes, but just in case.

Then do it. Agree on a time and place, organize transportation, if necessary, show up where and when you're expected, appropriately shod, and walk. If your companion is also new at this keep tabs on her energy level. I keep my eye open for benches and other potential sitting places and suggest a sit down after a half mile or so, or maybe 15 minutes. After you've caught your breath and taken in the scenery around you can decide together if you want to go on or go back. The slower, less experienced walker sets the pace. If she wants to turn around even though you could do another 15 minutes out, plus a half hour back, it's best to turn around. It takes time to build your stamina, don't push somebody else. I think back with gratitude at my earlier walk buddies, and how accommodating they were to my new-walker attempts.

If, on the other hand, your companion turns out to like a brisker pace than you're comfortable with, or walk further than you think is fun, speak up. "I don't think I can keep up with your pace, but if you'd like to walk ahead that would be fine." "I have my eye out for a place to sit down and catch my breath. Do you see anything?" She's not a mind reader and will probably be happy to go with your flow.

Patricia Beynen

Solo walks are good, companion walks are good.

Variety is good.

The Technology Option

Walking is just walking. No technology there. Some people use a treadmill, which is just a mechanical option, not very techy. I don't mean that.

Do you already have earbuds and listen to podcasts? You can skip this chapter. But that wasn't me. I didn't know how to do it, in spite of grandchildren telling me there was nothing to it. Uh huh. I knew what a podcast is. People talking on a topic, which is recorded and available to be downloaded. I get that. But, uh, how? And what then? With what? And how does it apply to walking.

As directed by my younger generations I found earbuds on Amazon. I already had a few sets of earbuds on wires around the house, but they fell out in a minute, no matter how carefully I placed them in my ears. I needed the kind that looked like old-style hearing aids, without wires. Bluetooth they told me. I found a bunch, picked a pair on the low end, and they arrived a few days later. I had to set my phone to synch them, which was just a single click under settings, and I was ready to listen.

But listen to what? I'm an NPR listener, so I could always choose to do that while I walking, but I wanted to try something new. I went to the Play Store on my phone, typed in Podcasts, found podcasts for android. Apple people would have gone to the Apple store on their phone and found something similar for Apple. I picked one called Podcast App which seemed appropriate. Clicked on it when it appeared on my screen, found a few podcasts that fit what I liked, and I was in business. Now I have a list to select from, depending on mood, and am now incredibly cool.

I listen while I walk now, but only when I walk alone. Today I listened to a discussion between two historians about the way we as a country have historically handled winning and losing. Their opinion was that after the Revolution we did a very decent job, much thanks to Alexander Hamilton's point of view, but after the civil war we did a poor job of reconstruction that led to many more problems. By the time we got to how we integrated German scientists into our space program after WW II I was home.

I walk farther when I'm listening to an interesting discussion. Although in general I don't find walking boring, it is more interesting while someone is talking to me, either the human next to me, or the voice in my ear.

Patricia Beynen

I think less about my feet and legs and lungs and more about the issue being discussed. It reminds me of my mother listening to the radio while doing a pile of dinner dishes as I dried. The radio made it go more quickly.

Years ago. I had a job that involved a lot of driving around a beautiful state. Beautiful, and large. It took a long time to get from one place to another, and I found that if I listened to books on tape, it made the time go much faster. Same principle here, and you can still listen to books through that earphone if that's your preference in listening. Download and listen. If it's not totally clear how to do that ask for a demonstration from a tech-competent eleven-year-old. They'd be glad to help. At least my grandchildren are always helpful, and nice about it too.

Even though two earphones arrived in the nice recharging itself box, I only wear one. I don't want to be cut off from the sounds around me. The other ear keeps me in touch with my surroundings, which seems like a smart thing to do. Don't be oblivious to where you are, or what's going on.

Patricia Beynen

Set Some Goals

Perhaps you already have a goal in mind, an end state you want to get to. For instance, I find it quite lovely to walk along the shore at the water's edge, but until recently I also found it more tiring than I wanted. I'd walk for fifteen minutes or so, then need to sit for a bit before I could walk back. My goal was to walk up and back to the pier without needing a rest.

Perhaps your goal is the number of steps in one outing. That outing could include a few minutes on a park bench, but it's the number of steps that you're after, without regard to length of time.

Or maybe you think a brisk walk right after breakfast is ideal. Thirty minutes total, fifteen out, fifteen back, done, and you have the day in front of you.

Or maybe you have progressive goals, say to add 250 steps a day to your goal every week. You're building your stamina, seeing a difference, and not killing yourself in the process.

Or maybe it has nothing to do with distance and stamina, but you build your walks around what you want to see. Residential areas outside of your normal boundaries, walks with friends in their favorite places, destination walks like the library or a new coffee place. I have driven down streets, getting a glancing look at houses that look surprising or interesting, but not able to take in any details. You could always drive to that area and walk a loop from your car, down fascinating street one, up fascinating street two, and back to your car. The goal was to see something new, and you did it.

Distance, steps, time, destinations are all good ones, but the biggest motivator may be keeping up with a friend or family member who you would like to spend some time with. However, you were out of sync with their pace, and didn't want to hold anybody up. You may find that you're getting to be such a successful walker that they are trying to keep up with you. Not a competition of course, but perhaps a tiny ripple of satisfaction.

Watch Your Feet

Yesterday I came home from walking aggravated at sidewalks that are nearly unwalkable, the ones that force you into the street, or across to a more accommodating sidewalk.

These come in two distinct categories: the runaway tree, and the overgrown walkway. I was so annoyed I became hyper aware of them, knowing that they could cause me to fall at any moment.

I did fall a few years ago when walking to catch a train in my own neighborhood, on the main commercial street. I blame a tree that was no longer there. The sidewalk bulged up and uneven over roots from a tree that had already died and been cut down, but left its remnants behind. I had walked that stretch many times but this once I wasn't paying enough attention, didn't lift my feet enough, and was down flat on my face, breaking a wrist on one side and the upper part of my arm on the other. As the ER doc said, it could have been worse, I could have had a concussion, but somehow my forehead ended up on my purse which flew in front of me when I stuck out my arms to catch myself. So, you see, I know from falling, and don't want to do that again. Hence, tree and sidewalk vigilance.

The tree hazard is all about the roots that grow higher than the sidewalk that is over them. They tilt the slate, bulge the concrete, or dislodge the bricks. An accident waiting to happen. The thing is, though, that it doesn't have to be that way. I also pass lots of examples of trees domesticated into their sidewalks, maintaining a walkable surface, Why, oh why, aren't they all like that?

The other hazard is the overgrown area. Sometimes it's right in front of a house and is just poorly tended. Sometimes it's a vacant house where no one is paying any attention. Or a vacant lot which is overgrown everywhere, right up to the street. Special mention to those houses that have a well-manicured and walkable front sidewalk, but the lot goes all the way through to the street behind them where they consider that the back 40 and let nature take its course. These paths only get worse as leaves fall, it's all trampled into slime, and freezes. With an uneven walkway underneath. Worst Case Scenario.

Which brings us to the ice, and snow. Beware. Issues are one part winter footwear, one part shoveling and salting by the owner, and one part quality of the surface to begin with. It's treacherous out there, and a good idea to stay away from the places you already

know have lurking tree roots and an uneven surface. Use

your judgement about walking through new snow on

good, well-known walkways. You might want to wait for

the salt and shoveling to do their jobs.

Make a Chart

For some of us it didn't happen unless it made it onto the chart. For others such things are met with a shudder.

If you're shuddering right now, feel free to skip the whole chart idea, or maybe do the stripped-down version of writing whatever you're keeping track of on the calendar, and you're done with it.

But, my fellow chart people, we can track, color code, use different fonts, and calculate averages on our charts. Won't that be fun?

In Excel, that grandmother of all chart making aps, it's all straightforward if you've spent time in a work setting doing fancy charts with macros and formulas to track finances and production and resources.

Patricia Beynen

I've forgotten all the fancy stuff, but I can still put
together something simple.

First decision is what do you want to track, the
easiest being time, steps, and/or distance. Do you want to
be reading across rows, or down columns? You might as
well put all three items in, and use what you want on any
given day. If you're interested in next level stuff, like
averages for a week, leave space for that. If you have a
specific goal, you could make a column for that and
indicate progress, like, say, your goal is 5000 steps a
day, and you're now doing about 3000, you can show
how you're closing in on the goal.

If you think it's a grand idea to record all that,
but have no interest in developing a chart, or using a
computer to enter the numbers, I've included a model at
the end of this book for you to copy. There's a blank

column for you to add whatever you like. My walking ap includes calories used as a statistic. Maybe you want to include that.

The goal of all this is to see progress, or, if no progress to see why not. Are you skipping too many days, is your step count going down? Maybe your notes section tells you it rained for five days straight, or alternately told you that 8000 step day was the day you walked with a friend. You were having such a great conversation that you walked for an hour hardly noticing the distance. Measuring tells you a lot, but so do the notes.

Patricia Beynen

Skip Days

The day arrives when you have other things on your calendar, the weather is lousy, or walking seems like a not-great idea. Allow yourself those days, within limits. Preferably not two in a row, or more than two a week.

You've been working to establish a habit of walking, something you can do without too much effort or planning. It seems like creating a habit takes intention and attention. Losing the habit is much easier…forgetting your intention and attention. Two days turn into four, and pretty soon you go a week without getting out there. Be conscious of what you're doing, and especially, not doing.

But sometimes, sure. You're the boss of you. I especially felt that way yesterday. We were meeting family for lunch, which was a long one. On the way home we went to the grocery store, that many-aisled emporium of temptation. I walked every aisle, so that was something. I had also parked at the almost-farthest end of the lot, so there was that. I hadn't taken a morning walk, so unless I decided to get it together late in the day, this was it. Turns out, that was it, totaling about 1500 steps. It could be worse.

In retrospect, I should have gone out first thing 7:30ish. I had a zoom call at 10, so it required a more intentional morning. Oh well.

So, today, for sure, at least 1500 steps.

Patricia Beynen

The Camera Walk

Now that we all have cameras in our pockets it's fun to look at the world through camera eyes. What would that doorway look like as an isolated picture? What about a lot of doorways? Document away.

Any anomaly is worth capturing. A strange bug, the first lilac, a cat in the sun. It sharpens your gaze to imagine something that is a detail as the focus of a photo. Take the picture, you can always delete it later.

We are having a building boom in my neighborhood. A store that's been empty for years is being torn down and a mid-rise apartment is shown on the sign in front of the construction fence. I pass several examples within only a few blocks, and I take pictures to show the original lot, and document progress. Or a vacant lot can become a building site overnight, sometimes to the complete surprise of even the nearest neighbors. Picture worthy.

I come upon unexpected things that I like to capture. Like a small sitting area set up for public use by neighbors at the end of a one-way street. Delightful. A double house with structurally identical sides owned by two separate entities, and each side displays its own taste, budget, and color choices, usually with no regard to the other side. The worst taste and color clashes are the most interesting.

Living in an historic area of an old city is full of opportunity for pictures. An old Friend's cemetery with no headstones, only plaques in the ground, is full of names that match street names and old factories. My favorite thing to keep an eye out for is often well hidden, and I when I find one, I feel like I've ripped away a hundred and fifty years to see what life used to look like. I'm talking about carriage houses. Sometimes they've been repurposed into apartments, or garages. A few are falling down, but nearly all are built of stone from local quarries and the roof is the only vulnerable part. They are windows on the time when horses were transportation, not a leisure activity, that people had different skill sets than we did, where the line between "women's work" and "men's work" was sharp. Where these big houses were run by "the help" not the homeowners. One or two that I've seen are short-term rental units for visitors who want a different experience. They're always charming, with patios and flowers, barely visible behind the house, down the driveway. But I see them, and take their picture.

The Exchange Walk

When I hear a disparaging comment about my neighborhood, I am always shocked. Really? You think that?

The commercial areas are not what they once were, but the housing is still pretty great, at least to me. Why would someone think otherwise? As I was walking down one of these old streets, I was thinking that the people who say "You live in Germantown, really? Do you feel safe?" should walk with me and see what I see. Which led to an idea.

I probably have ideas about their areas too. Too snobby, or kid oriented, or expensive, or new, or whatever I'm not liking at that moment. But I should probably walk through their neighborhoods before I give any opinions at all.

So, I emailed a friend and proposed exchange walks. One morning in my neighborhood, one in hers, to be followed by coffee at someplace along our paths. Done. She liked the idea too. As a fellow walker, with whom I've taken many city strolls and park walks I knew she was open to a few thousand steps in most places. We arranged the times, and made it happen.

Two slices of Americana, both filled with sights to remember. I quite loved her area, filled with well-tended 20th century houses, pretty gardens, school buses picking up kids, other walkers, especially dog walkers, and parks. It was a delight, and we talk talk talked our way through 3,000 steps. She liked mine too, with unexpected grandeur, steep hills, and a huge park that even had coffee available, sold out of a garage window, and enjoyed at picnic tables.

Thus, the neighborhood exchange walk was born. I've seen some lovely suburbs, neighborhoods, retail/condo/park locations and found a cup of coffee everywhere. I give choices for local walks here: the big park with trails, down to the pond and around, through the University, to the historic area, or all houses. There are four possible coffee endpoints, and sometimes the choice is based on coffee, or combos of the views, the sidewalk conditions (I agree, some are awful) and the break for coffee location. We could mix those factors forever and have walks and walks. Another way to encourage ourselves to get out there and walk.

Patricia Beynen

When You're Away from Home

Being away from home seems to automatically add steps to my day. The getting there requires some movement, and then being outside of your normal space usually means more walking. Lots of choices present themselves, like incorporating walking in the trip itself, parking farther away, or getting off public transit at an earlier or later stop than usual. If you're flying, you'll get a lot of steps in whether you want to or not. Why does your gate always seem to be the one farthest from the TSA screening? Not to mentioned the unplanned treks when there's a gate change, or the quest to find a bottle of water.

But say you're on an overnight visit, staying with your daughter's family. A normal visit, in non- pandemic days, might involve lingering around the breakfast table,

taking in one of the grandchildren's events, perhaps a

meal out, maybe a movie together. Perhaps a little

shopping. If you've been less sedentary since your last

visit, they might be surprised to hear you suggest a walk.

Surprised and pleased. Walks are free, can be started

right out the front door, and are a pleasant event to do

with one person or more. This allows the

host/hostess/grandchild to show you some highlights of

the neighborhood you may never have noticed from a

car. Look for ways to use your other new

tricks…walking to destinations instead of driving,

parking farther way, walking for entertainment and

companionship, listening to podcasts, books, and talks

with earphones if you're on your own, focusing on

particular elements you see as you walk and deciding

your preferences, and using your camera to memorialize what you're seeing.

But, say you're visiting an unfamiliar place, like a city that's new to you. All of the above, plus look for indoor walking options like museums and malls, or sports arenas if you're so inclined. It's been years since I've been to a baseball or football game, but I remember there was a lot of walking involved.

Perhaps your destination is in the country. A lovely inn, with tea by the fire. Before you get your tea reward, consider a country walk, either a trail or just down the road and back. Or around the grounds if it's a resort.

If, lucky you, you are near a body of water there are sure to be places to walk, if only back and forth to the water. If there's a boardwalk, take advantage. If there's a walkable shoreline, get your feet wet and walk

in the water. Maybe there's a small downtown with a

few restaurants, some shopping, a salon, a bookstore,

and ice cream. Walk the distance, see what there is.

Walking will show you so much more than observing

from a car, and lets you stop and get a better look

anytime you want.

You'll see both new and familiar places with new

eyes if you've never seen them on foot before.

Patricia Beynen

Walking with the Frail Elderly

It's not quite the same.

Perhaps you've seen people walking around retirement homes with a cane or a walker. You've gotten an impression…really old (or at least ten years older than me), slow, using assistance either human or something to hold on to. What did you think?

A lot of us think "why bother?" Wrong thought. Whether you're three or 45 or 75 or 96 walking is still a good thing. It revs up parts of the body that have just been sitting there, including the mind. It improves the appetite for the next meal, and the quality of sleep later on. It's worth the bother.

But, some forethought, please.

Falling, and fear of falling are the worries. Scope out the path you'll be following for any hazards, like wet leaves and mud, debris from a storm, or anything that will make you leave the path. Figure out your solutions before you head out.

Another is distance. You don't want to find out that dear Ms. Abby can only go about 500 steps without being exhausted after she's already walked the 500 steps. Inquire about how far she has gone before, or do a trial walk of, say, 250 steps, then turn around. In good shape? Ready for more? Another lap. Notice when she starts to tire. You don't want to be at the far end of your walk when exhaustion sets in. You match your pace to her slower one, no sprinting ahead.

Look for resting places, like a bench, or a low stone wall in a pinch. You can plan those in as recovery sites. Or, bring your own resting place by pushing a wheelchair to be used just for a sit down, or for a ride back.

Come prepared with good chat. A whole story, start to finish, about what happened when you shopped for a new outfit, or when you couldn't find the cat for a whole day and every place you looked. If you're walking with someone in your family you have a whole cast of characters to discuss. Perhaps a former neighbor? Topic A will be what's happening on the street, especially with her old house. The upcoming election? A good Netflix binge? All fodder for your walk.

If your companion is up to walking and talking at the same time, give her the chance to spill. You may find out something interesting. If walking with no talking is more her style, be sure to give her a chance to talk when she's on the bench for a refreshing rest. Ask a leading question if needed. Most people want to be heard.

Good for both of you. You for being there, helping hand at the ready, and her for still being in the game, getting up and out.

Patricia Beynen

The Awe Walk

I read about this, but since I found out it had a name, I haven't experienced it.

Awe: *A positive emotion elicited when in the presence of vast things, not immediately understood.*

The idea is that when walking in the presence of these vast things, I'm assuming in nature, but maybe more, the awe you feel is so positive it overcomes whatever negative emotions are acting on you at that time. Combined with the positive aspects of walking itself, and especially if done with other people, there are measurable positive results.

It's not that I haven't been awed. Have you been to the Grand Canyon? Even more awesome than I could have imagined. But it wasn't part of a walking adventure so that doesn't count.

I don't think you need the Grand Canyon, though, to be awed. Sunsets, mountains, rivers, oceans, even not-so-nice things like floods and tornados can leave you awed.

This may be my next walking goal. Living in a city, the pieces of nature we see are not on a grand scale, and even sunsets don't get the long vista they deserve. But it's not impossible. Maybe a walk along the river with an overlook that shows a distance. Or a trip to the shore for a beach walk. Not impossible, just needs some planning.

I used to live in the Midwest where sunsets were spectacular, and seemed to go on for a long time. Here in the city, I get beautiful historic houses and brick sidewalks, but not much can hold a candle to walking along a farm road toward the sunset on an Iowa evening. Awe-inspiring.

The Cemetery Stroll

A very Victorian thing to do. They even brought picnics.

I've done several, sans picnics. It is a stroll, and a slow one at that. There's so much to read, and then puzzle out. Family groupings, with generations in the same plot; faded carvings, sometimes too faded to read; even some competitive mausoleums.

Where I live, we have one particularly old cemetery, or burying ground as it's called, where some of the American soldiers from the Revolutionary War were buried after the Battle of Germantown. The Brits won that one, under General Howe in case your history knowledge is a little blurry. The place is full, and is less than a square block in size, but it has some dedicated helpers and is part of an historical legacy group of buildings and sites so it gets some attention. They give occasional guided tours. The gravestones are eroded and difficult to read, but there is a map, and the stroller can figure it out. An experience for sure.

The big cemetery is a monument to excess in several areas. "These people had money!" it fairly shouts. Big, elaborate, spacious, and to our more modern eyes, ostentatious. But the Victorians liked a lot of frills in their living rooms, dresses, and it turns out, their resting places. Angels were popular, especially angels with trumpets. The super-rich of the day had mausoleums built along their own streets on the grounds, and you see names of the barons of 19th Century commerce. Those were Philadelphia's glory days and money was no object.

So, you walk around, reading the names, recognizing some, up and down some steep hills. You may have opinions about the taste of the day, but understanding that someday whatever we think is tasteful and appropriate will be dismissed and laughed at also.

So many infant and child deaths, along with so many maternal and infant deaths. I think grateful thoughts about modern obstetrics and the elimination of so many diseases and antibiotics. We live in a better, healthier world than they did, current pandemic notwithstanding.

I found a new area, totally different than the rest. Rolling green hills, wildflowers, all natural. A lovely place to walk, and according to a plaque, the site of their "green services" where everything, and everyone, is biodegradable. It is pretty.

You can clock a lot of steps in a cemetery, climb some hills, and ponder life's stories, but it won't be fast. Truly a place to slow down and smell the flowers.

The Excuse Page

Why I don't want to walk today	What to tell yourself
1. I'm tired. I stayed up too late	Walking will wake you up, make you more present in your day.
2. It's too hot	Start early, when it's cooler. Bring water.
3. I have a headache	All that good oxygen will clear your head and make you feel better
4. I'm in a bad mood. Nothing sounds good.	A nice mood enhancing walk is the answer. A well-known benefit
5. I'm bored with walking in my neighborhood	Fine. Walk someplace else. Another neighborhood, in a park, downtown, in a different town.
6. I'm a slow walker, nobody wants to walk with me.	If you're new at this, your pace will probably pick up, so keep at it. If you've reached a pace that's as fast as it's going to be, make podcasts your friends

	and listen while you walk. Or try some peppy music to change your pace.
7. I have too much to do today.	Really? None of that is timewasting stuff like playing word games or staring at your phone? If the day really is that packed, get up a half hour earlier and walk for fifteen minutes. The walk will give you more energy for the things you need to do.
8. I'm going out with a friend today, no time.	Sure, there's time. Walk with your friend at least around the block and catch up before you launch into the planned activity.
9. My feet hurt.	Why do they hurt? Fix the problem if possible. Medical intervention, different shoes, orthotics. It's worth the trouble to find the answer.
10. It's too cold.	Bundle up. The walk itself is warming.

	Walking in the cold is the only time I actually like wearing a mask.
11. I'm going on a trip.	For a car trip, walk around whenever you get gas or stop to eat. For planes and trains walk around the airport or station while you're waiting. Look for walk opportunities everywhere. You are not helpless.
12. I have physical limitations	Talk to the doctor. If a physical therapy prescription is in order, that can help a lot. Consider walking aids like canes and walkers. Some walking is better than none, do your best
13. I have a book/Netflix series/project I want to finish	Nice. Walk first, then do it.
14. I'm too fat	All the more reason to walk. It burns calories, but it is harder with extra weight to carry around. As you lose weight it will get

	easier, and walking is part of that process.
15. I get out of breath	Plan some rest stops to catch your breath and start back.
16. I'm afraid of falling	A cane can steady you even if you don't use it in everyday life. Or a walking stick, which is taller can create the third leg for balance. Walk with another person if the concern is keeping you from even starting a walking experience.

Forest Bathing

The Japanese Ministry of Agriculture, Forestry and Fisheries named the concept in the '80s, although it was probably practiced for a long time before being officially recognized as a good way to spend time. Forest bathing is promoted in Japan as an antidote to the stressful, fast pace of business and urban life.

It's defined as the practice of immersing yourself in nature in a mindful way, using your senses to derive the benefits to your physical and mental health.

No picture taking, no thought of a step count, just awareness of the forest around you. Full attention. Submersion into it all.

The intent is to free you from all the stresses of life, for a little while. To allow your body first, and then your mind to relax by breathing in the smells, feeling the textures, hearing the sounds, seeing the flora and fauna, and tasting the air.

It means not just to be in the forest, but to take it all in, using all your senses. Really be there. I've seen several ways that the stages are defined, but here's one.

1. Be fully present. No phones, step counters, music, podcasts, or chatting with another person. No distractions.

2. Wander. No agenda or goal except breathing and being aware.

3. Notice small things, like a leaf or an aroma, maybe a rock. Stop and take a good look.

4. Have a seat. What's going on around you? Birds singing? Leaves rustling? Does your

presence change things? Does it change back after a few minutes?

5.   If you came with other people, regather outside of the quiet and share your experiences. If you came alone think through what just happened.

6.   Consider writing down your observations of what your perceived both outside and inside yourself.

To do that you need to shed some items usual in our lives, like electronics, and efficiency. There's no timetable, no prereq.

The ideal is a true forest, but an urban park will do. Try to be there for at least twenty minutes, but stay as long as you'd like. You want to shed stress, not add to it.

There's no end goal to this walk. Roam at will. Stroll in the direction that interests you. Sit when you want. Stay as long as you'd like. Eyes and ears open, relaxed breathing.

People with Disabilities

The disability community is a lot of people, dealing with diverse issues. Some are new to the challenges; some have lifelong skills and could write their own books about overcoming barriers. This is just a corner of what the full picture would reveal.

If you can get out there and walk, it's still worth it. Every time I read a list of the benefits of walking, I see one more. Today I read that walking can keep your ears from getting clogged with wax. Can you imagine? Walking? But there you are.

Surfaces are important. What feels the most stable for you is important, whether that's unpaved earth which may be easiest on the joints, or indoor floors that are reliably even. It's useful to pay attention to which works best for you, and what particular hazard makes it more difficult.

What's your energy level? Pick your path with that in mind. Hills use more energy, and trying to match your pace to a faster-walking companion can be exhausting.

Don't rule out winter. Try getting traction cleats for your shoes. They slip over your shoes to give you traction on snowy, slippery surfaces. These aren't cleats like golf cleats, but coils to give your walking more stability. Cleats come in bigger versions for ice climbing, but that's overkill for a simple walk around the block. They'll provide some stability and make a slippery sidewalk less slippery.

Trekking poles can also be helpful. They're usually adjustable in length, and provide upper body movement as well as giving you better balance. Have you heard of "Nordic Walking?" Picture striding along, with a walking pole in each hand. It started as a Finnish sport to make walking a more full-body experience. It's now an actual sport enjoyed all over Europe. It can also be enjoyed by anyone who wants to walk but is concerned about their stability and balance.

Consider some of the barriers that might be keeping you from setting out to walk. Perhaps:

- The distance of the walk, or roughness of the terrain.
- Your ability to keep up with companions and feeling unhappy that you're slowing people down.
- Your own resistance to using an assistive device.

- Fill in your own barrier next...

Each one seems to have a built-in answer once you've recognized it as the obstacle. You can determine the length of the walk, or the terrain you're walking on. Let your walking companions know that you'd enjoy spending time with them, but your pace is going to be slower and the walk may be shorter. Would they prefer to slow their own pace, or meet you at a predetermined rendez-vous place? Bring whatever assistive device works for you and use it. Was it a secret that walking is difficult for you? Your triumph is that you're doing it at all.

Many people report that their physical therapist has been instrumental in getting them out and about. If balance, chronic pain or gait issues are holding you back, ask your doctor for a prescription for PT, even if you've been through a course of treatment before.

If you'd like to walk with someone else but don't currently have that person available considered joining a local Disabled Meetup Group. They have scheduled activities and the people you meet might be interested in joining you for a walk.

Even though we're talking about walking here, if you're in a wheelchair consider spending more time outside, either in a "forest bathing" kind of way, or covering the ground while in your chair. We more able-bodied folks would honestly be delighted for your company.

Patricia Beynen

Perils and Good Things

It's all a balance, right? How much sleep, how many calories, organizing social interactions, being present as a spouse, parent, friend, neighbor. One big balancing act. You, as a thinking person, consider the options, and choose.

I actually couldn't think of too many perils associated with walking, but maybe you have your own list. Here's mine:

- Idiot drivers. Honestly, the way they barrel around a corner or ignore a stop sign is a peril to any pedestrian. Be on the lookout.

- Tree roots, whether growing on their own through an unpaved path or bumping up a slab of sidewalk, they really do seem out to get you. Beware. Strengthen those leg muscles, lift your feet, watch what's in front of you.

- Doing too much too soon. If you've been sitting in your recliner making no unnecessary movements for quite a while you are providing quite a shock to your body. Take it slow, literally. Consider a gentle stretch first. This is not a dash, it's a walk, at your speed. Not too far, not too rugged, just right. Build from there.

- Bad actors. That's what they call bad guys now. The kind that jumps in front of you and demands your wallet, or worse. Have a care, folks. Think daytime, well-traveled area, not going into the woods alone. Don't flash your diamonds either. Preventive action.

But! The good things! So many.

- Walking is the recommendation of choice for exercise from many a doctor. It's **good for so much of your body**, like: strengthening bones, building muscles, getting more vitamin D (from the sun), giving you an appetite for healthy food, tiring you enough to improve your sleep, and the many benefits that brings (like improved memory, better energy…). And the big one, lower mortality rates. Not to mention it also lowers incidence of glaucoma, reduces the incidence of getting Type 2 Diabetes, heart disease, and high blood pressure.

- **Mood improvement**: an overall feeling of evenness, perhaps more optimism, lessening feelings of tension and stress. Walking also seems to ward off depression, even producing a version of the runner's high after an hour of brisk walking. That's outside of our definition of genteel walking, but you might want to give it a try.

- **An idea factory**. No data on this, just a personal observation. I get ideas when I'm walking, alternative solutions to problems, fixing a plot tangle if I'm in the middle of writing something, better word choices when I'm stuck on a wrong word, thoughts about a new dinner to make, a trip to take.

- **Maintaining your own mobility**. Aging seems to be a lot about loss. If you have the option to keep or lose something as important as mobility, do all you can to keep it. Mobility and independence go together. You want both. Walkers are less likely to develop a disability like osteoporosis, and to heal more quickly from a disabling accident. (Feinberg School of Medicine, Annals of Internal Medicine)

- **A memory jogger**. Nothing like aromas to set off a memory. As I walk through

the seasons and see the progression of
flowers, the smells trigger other times
I've breathed that fragrance. Sometimes
it's to my great surprise, because I
haven't previously remembered that bush
that my father dug out of the yard when I
was nine years old, but there it is, and
okay, I remember now.

- **An occasion for social interaction**. Put
out the word that you've started some
neighborhood walks, and would be happy
for some company. The walk and chat are
their own reward, but coffee or lunch
could be the bonus round. Another
version is the interaction you have with

your fellow walkers or front yard gardeners as you encounter them.

- **An opportunity to know your home area better**. You see things when you walk you just don't see from a car. You can stop and puzzle out something that doesn't seem to make sense. You're and observer of new construction. You get to see all the tasteful and over-the-top holiday decorations. There may be streets you've rarely been down before, often because they're one way in a way that's not your way. And alleyways! Not all cities have them, but they can be pretty interesting, especially if they give you a view of backyards. Not to mention parks, those civic and "friends of" monuments to green oases in the city. Consider being a friend of your local park yourself, and show up with your gardening gloves and trowel on their volunteers' workday.

- As **part of a weight management program**. Mostly weight management is about calories in, but walking is a little bit of calories out. But only a little bit. According to my step tracker 5000 steps is only about 150 calories, but regular walking has more impact on shape than weight.

- **To be one with Thoreau** (from his essay Walking): *"No wealth can buy the requisite leisure, freedom, and* *independence, which are the capital in*

this profession."

- **Contributing to the greater good**.
Neighborhoods with walkers are safter
than those without according to the CDC

- One last, unexpected benefit to me.
Podcasts. For me, podcasts were a next
generation thing. My kids would quote
something they learned through a podcast
and I thought that was fine, but a younger
person thing, not my thing. With a little
younger person assistance, I downloaded
the app to my phone, picked a few that
sounded interesting and now I'm much
more knowledgeable about a lot of stuff. I
love Ted Talks. Remember, earphone on

one ear only. You want to hear what's

going on around you too.

So, eyes open, avoid the perils, and enjoy the

good things.

Patricia Beynen

What the Rich People Do

Have you heard of "throwing money at the problem?" That's what we say in my family when there's some issue we can't immediately solve. What do rich people do when their kid is flunking algebra, or the garden is getting tired looking, or you don't have a thing to wear. They throw money at the problem. The problem here being you, on the sofa or recliner, and not getting up and moving.

First, new clothes. You have to look good when you're out there, and Nieman Marcus has a special Stella McCartney collection for you. The female version of track suit top and bottom, cotton shirt, and shoes comes to $1605.00. You're going to look really good. For men, the price tag is a bit steeper at $6100 for the Stefano Ricci outfit.

Next you need a companion who will show up to make sure you actually going out that door. A paid personal trainer is just the ticket. To get one, google "walk companion personal trainer [your city name]" and you will be amazed. It turns out there is a whole universe of agencies, ala dating services, to find one. Wondering about the price? For someone to come to my door and walk with me for a one-hour session (the minimum) the price was $70 an hour, with a minimum commitment of 12 hours for three months. They would be happy to add extra services like nutrition planning or stretching exercises for $10 more an hour. I filled in a few basic facts with contact info and a description of my request and immediately got responses, including a zoom call to schedule a "fitness review" to determine exactly what I wanted. I scheduled the call and found out I could request the preferred gender of my companion, how much talk I wanted (silent, conversational, story teller…), and pretty much any other characteristic I could describe. I could schedule my 12 hours for one hour a week or more frequently. Other variations are possible as well, like twice a week then skip a week.

Now that you're all toned up and an experienced walker, it's time for your reward. Welcome to the world of Walking Vacations. Road Scholars offer several, for example Cinque Terre in Italy, exploring the "Five Towns" along the Italian Riviera, among Medieval fortresses, olive groves, and cliffs down to the Mediterranean. Expert lectures, hands on experiences plus food and lodging. Or perhaps the Cotswolds and

Cornwall in Britain? Or New Zealand? The choices go on. Or is walking in the US your pleasure? Cities, National Parks, you name it, there's a walking vacation already preplanned and waiting for you. The prices are all over the place depending on duration and services but $2000 a week, plus round-trip transportation, first class for, say, $6000-9000 per person.

And that, dear folks, is how the other half lives, or maybe now it's the one per-centers. But you can have many of the benefits of all this movement on an entirely different budget. Put together the clothes after shopping in your own closet, schedule regular walks with friends, and plan a walking tour of someplace you've been wanting to explore that is not so far from home.

Guided Walking Tours

After you've been walking for a while, you'll notice that it gets easier. If you're watching a step counter, you'll see that the numbers that used to exhaust you are now more routine. You might be noticing an entertainment option that previously escaped, the walking tour.

They range from around the neighborhood, guided by the local history buff who knows the history of houses, what was there before, some natural elements like a creek that used to be visible but now flows in a pipe, and the oldest and biggest tree in town. Some local walks are more focused on gardens, or maybe inside-the-house tours. Or beekeepers, or wildlife. So many types.

They usually last about an hour and a half, and you will learn a lot.

But what makes your part of the country special? We have lots of history here, so also have choices of historic walks, seeing the places where history happened. Where the Declaration of Independence was signed, where Betsy Ross sewed that flag, where George Washington lived with his family and enslaved staff. But more than that there are tours of how the city works, like the Underground Tour where you learn how the subways were built, and previously-unknown-to-you underground tunnels that trucks use to reach secret loading docks.

You never knew what you had been blithely walk over before. Perhaps a water department tour of the sewage plant. No kidding.

Patricia Beynen

Special walk for a rainy day: Go to your local museum, either art, historical, ethnic, or scientific. The tours are wonderful, and you'll learn more with a guide than just wandering on your own. Sometimes these places are a destination more than a local event. You'll find museums for dolls, farm machines, trains, specific artists, candy, quilts, and antique planes, to name just a few. A destination, a walk, and more knowledge than you ever imagined you'd have about a particular subject.

Go a little farther afield and look around the neighboring area. We have a wine tour only about half an hour a by car. You can tour the wineries, taste the varieties, and go home with your choices.

Prefer an art colony stroll? Nearly every area has one of those. Remember when just the thought used to exhaust you? You'd get so tired, parking would be farther away than you wanted, really you were there for the restaurant dinner. Now, with new eyes and energized muscles, you can appreciate all that art, from primitive and amateur to professional, and still get a good dinner whether it's in your own city or a car/train/bus ride away.

Nature walks are a big thing. Of course, you can do one anywhere, but State Parks usually have guided walks to show off their views and unique attractions. Experts with a passion about their subject will often be guides for wildflower walks, or on a riverfront, or to see butterfly environments. Google nature walks and your location…you'll see. Caution about the word "hike", as in "Nature Hike with Scenic Overviews". Personally, I think that's a bit much. Walk, that's the ticket. Flatter terrain, slower pace, chance to stop and smell the flowers.

Patricia Beynen

As hikes go, the granddaddy of them all is walking the El Camino de Santiago, the Way of St James. The 500-mile walk takes you through northern Spain, enjoying the culture, the comradery of fellow walkers, the beauty of the country, and the incredible challenge of the walk. Guided tours are available where all arrangements are made for you.

But this is for you. If you feel you're ready for the hiking world, give it a try. Don't sign up for a guided hike until you've walked some of those rougher environments with a friend for a few hours. Be ready to go several miles, and keep up with the regular hikers, with a minimum of rest stops. These are serious outdoor folks, and they walk briskly, reflecting years of experience. They wear boots, hop from rock to rock to get across streams, and don't give a thought to those

daunting uphill parts.

Patricia Beynen

You Live in the Land of The Car

If you're reading this and thinking, "Yeah, right, that all sounds fine if your world is sidewalks and public transportation and coffee shops, not so fine if getting anywhere involves a car, there are no sidewalks, people drive too fast, and the café in town does serve coffee, but that's miles away." The other version involves cities and towns with lousy public transport, which also mean you need cars to get anywhere and the environment is the opposite of pedestrian friendly.

What then? How do you make all this walking happen in a place where the car is king? Here's how.

1. The obvious: If you have acreage use it as your trail. Get to know it better, the borders, the middle, what's growing and living there,

how the changes in season change it. You

could be like some famous artists and

capture the same place in each season. They

did it in paint, but you can take photos if you

prefer.

2. Find the public space, the parks, the trails,

    and start there. If you can actually walk to it,

    bonus points, but you'll probably have to

    drive there. Try out a few walks, and pick

    your favorites, making the round trip, from

    getting out of the car to getting back in about

    30 minutes long.

3. Shopping can equal walking, especially in

    big box stores. Park far from the entrance,

    walk every aisle, 30 minutes will go by

quickly, but do a bit more since you'll be, you know, shopping too.

4. Walk the roads, carefully. Take a tip from the French, who walk a lot. They take one of those ubiquitous white plastic bags with them and wave it at hip height when a car is approaching. The theory is that it makes you more noticeable as your earth toned clothes fade into the earth toned side of the road. Fifty million Frenchmen can't be wrong. Or find another way to make yourself more noticeable, like reflective strips or bright clothing.

5. Look for sidewalks. If you have housing developments, you might have a

neighborhood with sidewalks. Give them a try.

6. If you live in the coastal urban version of this anti-pedestrian world all of the above could work, but add boardwalk and beach walking to your repertoire.

7. Notice where the runners run, and when. Maybe 6 AM is prime time for being out there. A daunting thought, but then you'd have the rest of the day free.

8. Take a look at the high school track. Is it open to the neighbors at non-school hours? It's a possibility. If you happen to have a college near you try them too. If they have a walkable campus do a walkabout and evaluate

Patricia Beynen

.

Enjoy your time under skies less polluted

than in the city, appreciating sunrises and

sunsets, and seeing rainbows from afar.

Did You Forget?

Today while I walked, I listened to a podcast where a woman with young children, a husband, a job, a house, and a thousand demands on her every waking moment was lamenting about her lot. She remembered a time in her younger life when she did other things, she played racquetball, was in a theater group, made cakes from scratch. She decided how she would use her time. Not anymore. Anything new that she wants to do means she needs to subtract something else. She didn't hate her life, she loved her family, was happy with her job, but it was all just so much.

I used to be her. I remember wanting to join a neighbor who took a morning walk, but the time wasn't available. While she was walking in the morning, I was getting children up and dressed and out the door, while also trying to pull together a professional enough outfit to get me through another day of work. Plus, all that other morning stuff. I remember the thought passing in my head: "Someday you'll have lots of time, and probably miss all this. But you will be able to go for a walk in the morning." The thought was probably less cogent, but that was the sentiment. Someday I'll have more time.

Someday is here. I have more time, and I also use it altogether differently, and at a different pace. I can design this phase of my life, within limits, pretty much the way I please. If I ever thought ahead to this elder phase, it was in terms of not doing what my mother or grandmother did. Or doing the same things, but differently. Now that I'm here, I look at how I can expand my universe to areas they might have never experienced, and do a few things that I put off.

The simplest of those put-off plans is the daily walk. When I started a more regular walking program I wasn't thinking in terms of deferred activities, just some rosy thoughts of "more active" and "use it or lose it." But I remember now, thanks to that podcast, that I really did want to lace up my shoes and start out onto the sidewalks, back there in that other state, and life. Now I do, and you can too.

Patricia Beynen

Appendix

A Walking Program, the First 30 Days

Let's assume the spirit is willing but the flesh is weak. You want to do this, you know you should, you're convinced, but how much, how far, when? If you're in a "just tell me what to do" mood, give this a try.

The goal is to spend 25 minutes a day, amounting to 150 minutes a week, out there, in motion. Keep an eye on those 150 minutes a week. If every day isn't going to work for you split up your 150 minutes differently, like three days at 30 minutes one day off, and then two more 30-minute days, and another day off. Do the math however you like, but get to the 150 minutes.

Maybe 15 minutes before breakfast and 15 minutes after lunch.

But that's the goal, and if you've been sitting, not moving, for some time now remind yourself it's a goal, not a first step, and give yourself time to get to it.

Do you know where you want to walk? Directly from your front door will be easiest for you to maintain. If you have a destination, like a park, consider the walk in three parts, just like an exercise class The warm up— your walk to the park, the aerobic part—a lap or two around the park, more briskly, and the cool down—a slower walk home. As you change your walks keep those three elements in mind. Warm up, aerobic exercise, cool down. Consider this progressively longer and brisker schedule.

- Week one: Warmup for 10 minutes, more briskly for 5, then cool down for 10 minutes
- Week two: Warmup for 10 minutes, briskly for 10, cool down for 5 minutes
- Week three: Warmup for 5 minutes, briskly for 15, cool down for 5 minutes
- Week four: Warm up for 5 minutes; walk briskly for 20, cool down for 5 minutes

At the end of four weeks repeat the plan for Week Four with that schedule for another month. That will give you 30 minutes a day, 150 minutes a week, achieved over five days. From there it's yours to play with. Add more days, but fewer minutes per day? You're probably going farther now than when you started. Ready to vary your route with some hills? Perhaps some unpaved terrain for different muscles and stress points. If you like your route, but want to vary it go the opposite direction, or the other side of the street or a different time of day. Add some internal loops, like going around a block you usually pass by, returning to your route one block farther along, but three more blocks walked.

For more exertion using the same path you could add hand weights of one or two pounds each, or a weight vest. Remember, though, that you're putting weight on your shoulders, which can be hard on people with back issues. Again, a chat with your doctor before you decide.

Make sure you're assessing your body responses. Expect to feel worn out in the beginning, but notice how it gets a little easier, how you can walk a little farther in the same time. Pay attention to your mood. Feeling more cheerful? A bit less gloomy about the state of the world?

That's the endorphins kicking in to your brain. "Walking Can Help Relieve Stress — Extension and Ag Research News (ndsu.edu)" Some North Dakota State University work has shown that *"walking promotes the release of brain chemicals called endorphins that stimulate relaxation and improve our mood. Walking does not have to be done at a fast pace to have stress-relieving benefits. Even a stroll at a comfortable pace promotes relaxation, studies indicate."*

You're now eight weeks into your walking program. Good for you! Your job now is to keep it up, find ways to keep it interesting (read this book!), and enjoy the benefits.

NOTES

Mayo Clinic Benefits of Walking: Walking: Trim your waistline, improve your health - Mayo Clinic

Older Americans Act: H.R.4334 - 116th Congress (2019-2020): Supporting Older Americans Act of 2020 | Congress.gov | Library of Congress

Thoreau's Essay on Walking Walking (thoreau-online.org)

Older adult exercises from the YouTube channel of the National Institute for Aging,   Go4Life Exercise Videos - YouTube

The Awe Walk

https://psycnet.apa.org/record/2020-69974-001?doi=1

Centers for Disease Control (CDC) Tips for Getting Your Steps In | DNPAO | CDC also links to and activities for people with physical disabilities.

The Surgeon General's report on promoting walking. Step it Up! The Surgeon General's Call to Action to Promote Walking and Walkable Communities (hhs.gov)

Mood enhancement and endorphin release through walking. Walking Can Help Relieve Stress — Extension and Ag Research News (ndsu.edu)

A few books and articles for inspiration and thought:

- The Flaneur, by Edmund White, Bloomsbury Publishing

- Walking: A Complete Guide to the Complete Exercise, Casey Meyers, Random House

- The Unbearable Smugness of Walking, by Michael LaPointe, The Atlantic, August 2019

- Walking the Camino De Santiago by Davies and Cole, Pili Pala Press

- Thoreau's essay on Walking: Walking (thoreau-online.org)

- Walk Away Anxiety. Prevention Guide, 2021, Hearst Magazines

Patricia Beynen

Date	Minutes	Steps	Walk Name	Companion

About the Author

Patricia Beynen lives, and walks, in Philadelphia, Pennsylvania. She also takes pictures while she walks, including the cover photo of her beautiful part of the city.

Writing is her third career, after spending years first as a social worker, and then in the corporate world. She and her husband Bert, and their two cats, Ritty and Meeneus, live in a crooked narrow house on a crooked narrow street, the kind found all over the city.

Patricia would greatly appreciate a kind review of this book on the Amazon book page site for *The Elder's Guide to Genteel Walking*. If you would like to get in touch, her email is patricia.beynen@gmail.com.

Patricia Beynen

Made in United States
North Haven, CT
06 October 2022

25081028R00085